SPORTS GREAT SCOTTIE PIPPEN

—Sports Great Books—

Sports Great Jim Abbott
(ISBN 0-89490-395-0)

Sports Great Troy Aikman
(ISBN 0-89490-593-7)

Sports Great Charles Barkley
(ISBN 0-89490-386-1)

Sports Great Larry Bird
(ISBN 0-89490-368-3)

Sports Great Barry Bonds
(ISBN 0-89490-595-3)

Sports Great Bobby Bonilla
(ISBN 0-89490-417-5)

Sports Great Roger Clemens
(ISBN 0-89490-284-9)

Sports Great John Elway
(ISBN 0-89490-282-2)

Sports Great Patrick Ewing
(ISBN 0-89490-369-1)

Sports Great Steffi Graf
(ISBN 0-89490-597-X)

Sports Great Orel Hershiser
(ISBN 0-89490-389-6)

Sports Great Bo Jackson
(ISBN 0-89490-281-4)

Sports Great Magic Johnson (Revised and Expanded)
(ISBN 0-89490-348-9)

Sports Great Michael Jordan
(ISBN 0-89490-370-5)

Sports Great Jim Kelly
(ISBN 0-89490-670-4)

Sports Great Mario Lemieux
(ISBN 0-89490-596-1)

Sports Great Karl Malone
(ISBN 0-89490-599-6)

Sports Great Joe Montana
(ISBN 0-89490-371-3

Sports Great Hakeem Olajuwon
(ISBN 0-89490-372-1)

Sports Great Shaquille O'Neal
(ISBN 0-89490-594-5)

Sports Great Scottie Pippen
(ISBN 0-89490-755-7)

Sports Great Kirby Puckett
(ISBN 0-89490-392-6)

Sports Great Jerry Rice
(ISBN 0-89490-419-1)

Sports Great Cal Ripken, Jr.
(ISBN 0-89490-387-X)

Sports Great David Robinson
(ISBN 0-89490-373-X)

Sports Great Dennis Rodman
(ISBN 0-89490-759-X)

Sports Great Nolan Ryan
(ISBN 0-89490-394-2)

Sports Great Pete Sampras
(ISBN 0-89490-756-5)

Sports Great Barry Sanders
(ISBN 0-89490-418-3)

Sports Great John Stockton
(ISBN 0-89490-598-8)

Sports Great Darryl Strawberry
(ISBN 0-89490-291-1)

Sports Great Isiah Thomas
(ISBN 0-89490-374-8)

Sports Great Herschel Walker
(ISBN 0-89490-207-5)

SPORTS GREAT SCOTTIE PIPPEN

Peter C. Bjarkman

—Sports Great Books—

ENSLOW PUBLISHERS, INC.
44 Fadem Road P.O. Box 38
Box 699 Aldershot
Springfield, N.J. 07081 Hants GU12 6BP
U.S.A. U.K.

Library of Congress Cataloging-in-Publication Data

Bjarkman, Peter C.
Sports great Scottie Pippen / Peter C. Bjarkman.
p. cm. — (Sports great books)
Includes index.
Summary: Looks at the career of this basketball star who, in spite of playing in the shadow of Michael Jordan, has become one of the greatest all-around performers in the sport's history.
ISBN 0-89490-755-7
1. Pippen, Scottie—Juvenile literature. 2. Basketball players—United States— Biography—Juvenile literature. [1. Pippen, Scottie. 2. Basketball players. 3. Afro-Americans—Biography.]
I. Title. II. Series.
GV884.P55B53 1996
796.323'092—dc20 95-51440
[B] CIP
AC

Printed in the United States of America

10 9 8 7 6 5 4 3 2 1

Photo Credits: Frank P. McGrath, Jr., pp. 8, 10, 12, 15, 19, 22, 27, 29, 40, 42, 47, 49, 51, 54, 58, 59; New Jersey Nets, p. 37; New York Knicks, p. 33.

Cover Photo: Marie S. McGrath

Contents

Chapter 1

Scottie Pippen, small forward for the Chicago Bulls, is one of today's brightest NBA talents. He is one of the flashiest stars in a popular sport that is now enjoying its most glorious era. Pippen has been named to the All-Star Game six times (once he was named MVP). He has been a first-team All-NBA defensive-team selection four times, and twice has been named to the annual post-season All-NBA team, which is made up of the top five players in the league. Yet Pippen has had the misfortune to spend seven of his eight seasons on the same team with Michael Jordan. The Bulls are seen as Jordan's team and not Pippen's, and Chicago is Jordan's city alone. When the Bulls won their three recent championships, Jordan—not Pippen—received almost all the credit.

The comparisons of Pippen with Jordan never stop. They did not stop even when Jordan temporarily retired in 1993. When the Bulls failed to win a fourth league championship in 1994, despite a brilliant season by Scottie Pippen, the talk was all about how Chicago could have won again if only Michael Jordan had still been around.

A triple-threat player, Scottie Pippen would become best known for his slashing drives to the basket.

Scottie Pippen joined the Chicago Bulls back in 1987 as an All-American from tiny University of Central Arkansas. It was immediately obvious, even during that 1987–88 rookie season, that Pippen was destined to rank someday among basketball's most illustrious stars. With numerous acrobatic moves to the basket and a reputation as an electrifying finisher once he approached the net, he was a player of almost unmatched offensive skills.

Yet few outside of the experts appreciated what a rare talent Pippen truly was. Among the fans, everyone who came to see the Bulls play at Chicago Stadium or watched them on television seemed geared to see only Michael Jordan. Soon after Scottie Pippen joined the Bulls, he found out that playing on the same team with basketball's greatest living legend can never be easy.

Pippen's talents have not gone completely unnoticed, of course. Many veteran observers of the NBA have, for several years now, seen Pippen as second in overall talent only to Jordan among all the pro basketball league's greatest stars. Frank Layden, who once coached the Utah Jazz and is now their team president, asserts that "Michael is the only one better than Scottie." Bernard King, one of the league's great scorers of the past decade, says that "there is simply nothing Scottie Pippen can't do." And former NBA great Bill Walton echoes their sentiments, calling Pippen today's second-best all-around ballplayer.

But the most lavish praise for Pippen's game comes from Jerry Krause, the general manager of the Chicago Bulls. Krause believes that Pippen, whose "tools just stun you," is still "just scratching the surface of what he can be."

Even Jordan himself has been quick to acknowledge his teammate's unmatched skills as a basketball player. "When Scottie was first drafted, I had never heard of him. After he joined us, it was obvious he had the ability; that he had immense skills. It was just a matter of [getting the] confidence that all great players have. Now he has that confidence and now he is a great star. He helps take a lot of pressure off me."

Scottie Pippen is not only a truly great ballplayer; he is also a remarkable team contributor. However, he has not always enjoyed being a second-line performer, playing under the huge afterglow cast by Michael Jordan. Quietly, he grew impatient for his own chance to lead. With Jordan's surprise absence and his own early-season successes in 1993–94, the Bulls' most underestimated star now seemed ready to burst

Michael Jordan did it all for the Chicago Bulls throughout much of the 1980s. Until Scottie Pippen and Horace Grant perfected their own games, though, the Bulls were never NBA champions. Jordan is quick to acknowledge Pippen's contribution to the team.

from behind Jordan's shadow. All that was needed was the proper stage for a coming-out party. That stage was set with the league's February 1994 All-Star Game in Minneapolis, Minnesota.

The 1993–94 season had opened with Michael Jordan unexpectedly abandoning the NBA scene. Jordan was apparently satisfied with his three championship banners and now wanted to try his hand at professional baseball. Suddenly Pippen was left to lead the Bulls alone. Pippen could at last seize his own share of the glory. When the league's best players gathered for the 1994 All-Star Game in Minnesota, Scottie Pippen was ready to make a clear and lasting statement. (That contest marked Pippen's fourth appearance in an All-Star game. He also later played in the 1995 and the 1996 All-Star Games.)

Arriving on the Target Center floor for pregame warm-ups, Pippen could hardly be missed. He was wearing special fire-engine red Nike™ shoes that seemed to proclaim that he was now demanding the full spotlight for himself. As action unfolded in the annual showcase exhibition contest, Pippen indeed seemed to be in that spotlight almost constantly. The 1994 All-Star Game was a fitting stage for the Bulls' new number-one man to control the action and claim his rightful spot at the head of the league's superstars.

Pippen was more than equal to the task and soon led a spectacular one-man assault on Jordan's relinquished crown. Performing a five-star solo act in the midst of a full stage of "prime-time players," Jordan's former understudy scored a game-high 29 points as he shot 9 for 15 and also grabbed 11 crucial rebounds. Pippen also fittingly sank a difficult baseline jumper with only minutes remaining in the contest to secure a 127–118 victory for his underdog East All-Star squad.

Scottie Pippen provides a little airborne magic of his own with a slam dunk Michael Jordan style.

This time around it was Scottie Pippen and not Michael Jordan who was the consensus NBA All-Star Game MVP. The mantle had been duly passed, and a new basketball superstar received well-deserved recognition.

Pippen's career had definitely turned a corner with the All-Star Game in Minneapolis. But would that corner truly take the league's most overlooked star in a new career direction? Or would it only lead in a circle back to the same dead end? After all, few NBA watchers expected Michael Jordan to remain in retirement very long. These skeptics would soon be proven right. When Jordan returned, however, would stardom have to be shared with a new Bulls hero named Scottie Pippen?

Chapter 2

Some super-talented athletes are huge stars from their very earliest years as junior high or high school players. Youngsters who can shoot baskets, run and jump faster and higher than all of their classmates, or slug and toss a baseball are often huge celebrities in town even during their earliest teenage years.

This is especially true of basketball, in which someone with unusual abilities can put his or her town and school on the map and make it a sure winner. Basketball is the one team sport that places emphasis on individual moves and one-on-one solo talent. Some athletes, like Moses Malone, Bill Willoughby, Darryl Dawkins, or Kevin Garnett, are so good they can step from the high school basketball courts right into the pro basketball arenas. Other school heroes become college stars before turning professional.

And then there are those basketball players, called late bloomers, who seem to arrive at stardom from out of nowhere. Their early talent is sometimes rough. They are role players and not stars on their school teams. A few even take up the

Even though he got a late start in basketball, Scottie Pippen would emerge as a genuine offensive superstar who could complement the great Michael Jordan and make the Bulls three-time NBA champions.

game late because they were not born or raised where basketball is a popular sport.

Scottie Pippen of the Chicago Bulls was indeed a late bloomer. Like Patrick Ewing, Pippen didn't dribble his first basketball until he had turned eleven. Although Scottie loved sports as a youngster, he discovered basketball relatively late. At first he threw only baseballs and footballs on the sandlots near his rural Arkansas home. Once he did find basketball, however, Pippen immediately fell in love with the fast-paced game. But even when he was shooting hoops on the local playground, there was nothing about his basketball play to suggest he would become an unusually talented star athlete.

Scottie Pippen was the last of twelve children born to Preston and Ethel Pippen in the small rural Arkansas town of Hamburg. There were already five boys and six girls in the family when Scottie arrived on September 25, 1965. Preston worked long and difficult hours in a local paper mill to support his growing family, and the work would soon take a heavy toll on his health. Ethel also had to work long, hard hours just to keep up the household and to raise and watch over a dozen youngsters. Respect for hard work was one lesson that Scottie Pippen learned early from his two dedicated parents.

Such a big family meant there would not be any luxuries for youngsters growing up in the Pippen residence. Scottie's parents could not provide expensive entertainment or expensive playthings. They did, however, provide him with something equally important. The youngest Pippen grew up with a built-in supply of playmates in his own household. With five older brothers and six older sisters around there was always someone to give the eager youngster instruction and competition on the playground. In his early teen years he spent countless hours with his brothers and other friends on the nearby Pine Street basketball courts.

One of Pippen's boyhood friends, Ron Martin, later remembered that as thirteen and fourteen year olds the boys played basketball late into the night all year round. They played until they would be thrown off the court near midnight for making too much noise, keeping neighbors from sleeping. But the next day they would always be back. And the games consisted of every kind of basketball variation possible. There were team games. But there were also one-on-one battles for hours at a time, during which Scottie and Ron and their friends pretended they were all great NBA stars playing in important championship games.

One thing that held Scottie Pippen back as a teenager was his small size. Ron Martin later remembered that Pippen had equal talent, but Ron was bigger and at first took advantage of his shorter playmate in one-on-one games. But it didn't last for long. Pippen soon developed enough playground skills to make the high school basketball team by the time he was a tenth grader.

But making the team and being in the starting lineup are two different things. His first year as a high school basketballer in his hometown of Hamburg would hold very few pleasant memories for Scottie. Although he was good enough after his long hours in the playground to wear a uniform and gain a spot on the team, he was neither big enough nor good enough to play on a regular basis. Game after game the youngster sat on the bench. He practiced with the team but he didn't really play for the team. His pride was wounded and he soon considered quitting the team.

Scottie suffered another blow as a high school freshman. Hardworking Preston Pippen suffered a stroke after years of wearing himself down with exhausting hours in the steaming factory. Scottie's father remained alive, but he was now paralyzed and could no longer speak. Scottie now began to lose some of his earlier enthusiasm for sports and again considered leaving the basketball team.

Basketball was no fun if you never got a chance to play. And Scottie Pippen had another sporting interest at the high school that seemed to bring him a good deal more satisfaction than riding the bench for the basketball team. During the fall football season, Pippen was the manager for the football team. This was a job with plenty of responsibility and plenty of opportunity to feel important. He took care of equipment, passed out towels after practice, chased loose footballs, and even assisted the coaches with the charts and statistics.

Pippen loved being football team manager. He didn't even mind that his responsibilities meant that he had to miss several weeks of basketball practice in early November at the beginning of his eleventh-grade season.

But Coach Don Wayne had different feelings on the matter. Angry that one of his players, even a bench player, would ignore his obligations to the team, Coach Wayne wanted to boot Pippen from the roster. When teammates pleaded with the coach to let the popular sub keep his roster spot for his junior year, he relented. But he was not entirely willing to forgive. Pippen again sat on the bench almost every minute of the season.

Coach Wayne was understandably upset with young Pippen. But he would later become one of the youngster's biggest supporters. Perhaps he was most impressed and finally won over by the apparent self-confidence of this bench player who eagerly returned for his senior season despite his lack of playing time as a sophomore and junior. He also was impressed with how much Pippen had improved through his summertime practice away from the gym. A short way into his

Though he spent much of his high-school basketball career riding the bench, Pippen would go on to provide the Bulls with high-powered scoring.

senior year, Pippen had earned a starting spot on the team. He still wasn't very big at only six feet, one inch, and barely over 150 pounds. But his ballhandling skills had improved enough to make him the team's starting point guard.

By the end of Pippen's senior year at Hamburg High School, Coach Wayne believed that his hardworking player deserved a chance to try his hand at college basketball. Scottie now loved the game more than ever and had decided he indeed wanted to play in college. The trouble was that no colleges had expressed any interest in a six-foot one-inch point guard with only one year's experience as a starter.

In a last ditch effort to help his dedicated student-athlete, Coach Wayne telephoned an old friend who was serving as head coach at the University of Central Arkansas. Wayne explained to Don Dyer that Pippen was perhaps not good enough to make his varsity team but had experience as a student manager and could help out as a part-time practice player. Coach Dyer was willing to take a chance on a team manager—especially one recommended by his friend—and he saw to it that a work-study grant was arranged to help Pippen pay for his schooling. Dyer was also willing to give Pippen a chance to practice with the team.

Scottie Pippen still believed in himself as a genuine basketball prospect, even if few others did. He reported to the Central Arkansas campus and began to work out with the team while handling his chores as manager. Coach Dyer soon had the pleasant surprise of discovering that the student manager he had taken sight unseen was actually the best player he had in his gym. Before his freshman year was up, Scottie Pippen had traded in his spot as a student manager for a seat at the end of the players' bench. As a skinny freshman, Pippen would appear in twenty games as a valuable reserve.

The jump from manager to player was followed by the

bigger leap from player to team leader. It was as a college sophomore that Pippen exploded onto the small college basketball scene. He scored 18.5 points per game, collected 9.2 rebounds, and handled the pressures of the point guard position. A point guard is responsible for dribbling the ball into front court, setting up plays, and making skillful passes to teammates with open shots. Pippen would also on occasion fill in as a shooting forward or a rebounding center. As a junior and senior he only got better. For his second full season he averaged just under 20 points each game and was selected as a small-college NAIA All-American.

It was not only the ballhandling skills that grew for Pippen but his physical stature as well. He had reported to campus in Conway, Arkansas, already two inches taller than when he had left high school only three months earlier. By his sophomore year in 1984 he had shot up to six feet five inches and a year later he had stretched out to six feet seven inches and now weighed over 180 pounds. One assistant coach at Central Arkansas observed that as much as Pippen grew, he never seemed to lose his coordination and never forgot the carefully practiced ballhandling skills he had learned as a smaller athlete.

Most college basketball fans had still never heard of Scottie Pippen. There were not even many basketball experts or professional scouts who knew anything about him. He had been playing for an unknown school with a small-time schedule. He wasn't seen on television and didn't play in the NCAA tournament. But Coach Dyer for one was already a true believer. And Pippen himself was now beginning to think that he might even be able to play pro-style ball. Even a few NBA insiders, like longtime talent scout Marty Blake, had begun to take a mild interest in the glowing reports about the underrated player from tiny University of Central Arkansas.

Scottie Pippen was relatively unknown during his years in college. His coach was a true believer though. Pippen was on his way to stardom in the NBA.

More believers were made during the NBA summer tryout camps. These are the gatherings in which pro scouts and coaches evaluate players for the upcoming draft of new talent. Such tryout camps are especially important for small-college players, or for those not constantly in the headlines as star players for major schools in major conferences. Here a player who has not previously been well scouted has a chance to showcase his talents for representatives of all the NBA teams.

Jerry Krause, the Chicago Bulls general manager, was especially interested in Scottie Pippen. Krause noticed Pippen above all the other prospects even before he saw him shoot the ball or play in a game: "He had the biggest arms I've ever seen, and I've always been very big on long arms and strong hands."

Krause was not the only one who sat up and took notice. It was at the summer NBA tryout camp in Krause's own backyard in Chicago, however, that Pippen especially showed his true talent to a major audience of basketball insiders for the first time. The best-kept secret in the world of basketball would soon not be much of a secret anymore.

Chapter 3

Scottie Pippen was discovered by basketball fans everywhere on NBA Draft Day in 1987. The unknown small-college prospect had already been discovered months earlier by the coaches and scouts and front office management of the Chicago Bulls. The Bulls management had decided that Pippen was indeed the player they wanted in order to start building a winning team around superstar Michael Jordan. To get him in a Bulls uniform, on the other hand, might take more than just a little bit of luck.

Krause was more than a little worried that the Bulls might not be able to land the player they really wanted. The Bulls had the eighth overall pick in the first round of the upcoming draft. But Krause knew that other teams had spotted Pippen in the tryout camps. Scottie's stock had risen, and there was a good chance that another club would already have selected him by the time the Bulls would have their opportunity to make a selection.

In order to grab Scottie Pippen before other teams could get him, general manager Krause had to make a deal. The

Seattle SuperSonics owned the fifth pick, and they wanted a player that was not as likely to be chosen in the first half-dozen selections. He was a tall center from the University of Virginia named Olden Polynice. A trade was quietly completed, and when the Sonics made their choice of players they took Pippen. They were of course selecting for the Bulls, though no one knew it at the time. Krause then selected Polynice for Seattle with the Bulls' eighth pick. An hour later, with the draft still in progress, the secret trade was announced. Both teams had the man they wanted. Scottie Pippen would be putting on the uniform of the Chicago Bulls.

The Bulls already had a superstar. They had the biggest superstar ever. But even with Jordan, they had not yet been able to challenge for a title. Chicago fans were getting restless with season after season of mediocre teams that finished low in the standings. They were tired of having a one-man team guaranteed to always finish far out of the running when the playoffs rolled around—even if that one man was the flashy Michael Jordan.

The Bulls under Krause had a long-range plan. They were determined to provide Michael Jordan with just the supporting cast he would need to challenge Larry Bird's Celtics in the East and Magic Johnson's Lakers in the West. Krause was determined it would be a cast that was good enough to win an NBA championship.

Scottie Pippen was the first step in the master plan of general manager Jerry Krause. The second step came on the very same draft day in June 1987. The Bulls had two first-round picks in this draft, and with their second selection Chicago gained another player they felt could solve their needs on the defensive end of the court. He was six-foot ten-inch forward/center Horace Grant, who had played at Clemson University in the powerful Atlantic Coast

Though Michael Jordan was a superstar, the Bulls hadn't won a championship until Scottie Pippen joined the team. Here, Air Jordan soars to the hoop while Pippen positions himself for a possible rebound.

Conference where Jordan had once played. Grant was a solid defensive player who could intimidate other teams' scorers and also help out by collecting many rebounds on opponents' missed shots.

This is how NBA teams try to build themselves into winners. The draft rewards those clubs with poor season records by allowing them to pick first among the top players leaving college. Teams that select wisely can often obtain a handful of new stars who will make them competitive in only one or two short seasons. And by selecting Pippen and Grant, the Bulls had indeed chosen wisely. The Bulls improved their record from 40 wins the season before Pippen arrived to 50 wins in Pippen's rookie year. The Bulls had their first winning season in seven years.

It would of course take some time for the new Chicago team to come together. But everyone around the league could see after the summer of 1987 that the Chicago Bulls were a more balanced team. Pippen could support Jordan's shooting and scoring, and Grant could get the ball for Chicago's high-scoring duo on the front line. Some veteran players were being added to the mix as well. Charles Oakley teamed with Horace Grant as a rebounding force in the front court. John Paxson provided steady guard play. Dave Corzine was a reliable if not overpowering center. And Jordan was seemingly better than ever now that he was freed from the burden of carrying the entire team on his back.

Pippen and Grant would combine to bring a special dimension to the Chicago team. They would also become the best of friends. In one promotion held by the Bulls a few years later, players would be asked to name one person they would like to take with them on a trip to the moon. Answers would be printed on the players' page in the team yearbook. Pippen was quick to name Horace Grant as his own choice.

Powerful Horace Grant was not only the Bulls rebounding and defensive force close to the basket, but he was also Scottie Pippen's closest friend on the team.

From the beginning Pippen's glamorous new job in Chicago would be both a golden opportunity and a terrible personal frustration. For one thing, the Chicago team didn't seem to be all that much better during his first two seasons. There would be 50 wins and a second place finish in the Central Division his rookie year and a better than .500 record a season later. That second season the Bulls would again be a fifth-place finisher. While post-season play improved, the team was still not ready to challenge for a championship.

Pippen himself would also break into the league rather slowly. His rookie year got off to a rather rocky start. Pippen and his agent, Jimmy Sexton, couldn't agree with his new team on the details of his first professional contract, and the rookie had to sit out part of preseason practice. This put the new player behind schedule in adapting to the more demanding game of professional basketball. Once he did join the lineup, Pippen would average only about 21 minutes of playing time per game.

Pippen's numbers were certainly not very impressive his rookie season. This was no hotshot prospect taking the league by storm the way Jordan had done only a few years earlier. He averaged only 7.9 points a game, shot with only 46.3 percent accuracy, and collected only 3.8 rebounds a contest. These were not impressive numbers for a future star expected to help lead his team toward a championship.

Yet the Bulls were not at all disappointed in their slow-starting rookie. The potential of their top draft choice was there even for casual observers of basketball to notice. It was certainly obvious to expert observers like Bulls assistant coach Phil Jackson.

Jackson observed Pippen's unlimited potential when he noted for one reporter that the rookie "could rebound yet still dribble the length of the court." Jackson continued that Scottie

Pippen "had those slashing sort of moves so that you knew he was going to be a very good player, only you didn't know just how good."

With Pippen and fellow rookie Grant leading the charge alongside Jordan, the Bulls as a team would improve by leaps and bounds. The team was the surprise of the league in the 1987–88 season, improving by ten wins over the previous season and moving from fifth to second place in the difficult Central Division. Pippen and Grant didn't set the league on fire with their own personal statistics. They were all that was needed, however, to light a fire under Jordan's game. With fifty wins, the Bulls trailed the talented Detroit Pistons by only four games in the race to lead the Central Division.

With added help from players like Charles Oakley, John Paxson, and Dave Corzine, as well as their rookies, Chicago would even hold their own in the 1988 NBA playoffs. First they whipped the Cleveland Cavaliers in a five-game first-round series, taking the deciding game in Chicago Stadium by six points. Then they fell to the Pistons in five games, but did manage to defeat the powerful Detroit team once on the Pistons' own home floor.

There would, however, also be one very big setback in all of this steady and rapid progress. This came when Pippen himself was suddenly slowed with a late-season injury. He would have to have surgery on his injured back during the off-season, and although the surgery was successful it meant a difficult period of rehabilitation for his damaged muscles.

Pippen would have to miss training camp in the fall. For the second straight season he would enjoy no benefit from preseason exhibition games. He also sat out eight games at the start of his second season. But this was just the final calm before the storm. Shortly after Pippen returned to the active roster in mid-November he finally made the starting lineup.

Pippen was getting off to another slow start, but it would be the last slow start of his career.

Jordan, by contrast, rolled on and on as only Michael Jordan could do. He won another scoring title, his third in a row. But Pippen's scoring numbers swelled as well. Jordan's teammate averaged 14.4 points per game in his second season of 1988–89. It was enough, at least when combined with Jordan's firepower, to keep the Bulls a dozen games above .500 for the entire season.

A better-than-.500 record, however, meant only that the Bulls would finish in fifth place in the very tough Central Division. But the team was nonetheless once again back in the playoff picture when post-season rolled around.

The Chicago Bulls were becoming a force to be reckoned with. This was altogether clear before the 1989 playoffs were finally over. They climbed through the first two rounds of post-season for the first time in fourteen years. They were in the conference finals for only the third time in team history and the first time since 1975. Pippen chipped in with some heavy scoring, including 3 three-point buckets in a single quarter in the opening playoff game against Cleveland.

But the Bulls were still not ready to handle the rough defensive style of the Pistons, who were on their way to a championship of their own in 1989. The Bulls forced a sixth game in the conference finals series with Detroit. But then an elbow from Piston Bill Laimbeer sent Pippen out of the contest and the Bulls were again a beaten club. They lost 103 to 94 on their own home floor with a wounded Pippen sitting on the bench. It had been the best season in years, but suddenly yet another season was over without a taste of championship play.

A trip into the conference finals did accomplish one thing, however. There was now much optimism among Chicago's

Phil Jackson, who was an important back-up player for the New York Knicks, replaced Doug Collins as Chicago's head coach in 1989.

NBA fans about the upcoming 1989–90 season. Jordan was still healthy. Pippen was maturing and getting better and better all the time. And the supporting cast of Bill Cartwright, Paxson, Grant, and others was in place and even fine-tuned during the previous year's league action.

Another important change had placed Phil Jackson in the head coaching position. Jackson had been given the position after Doug Collins had difficulty in getting along with star players like Jordan and Pippen. But the coaching change did not seem to disrupt the Bulls' building momentum. Once again the Chicago team would find its way into the conference finals and a rematch with Detroit's Pistons. This time they would push the defending NBA champs all the way to a seventh game before being beaten, rather badly, in the deciding contest.

But the real story of 1989–90 was perhaps the next step in Pippen's march toward superstardom. Jerry Krause was one of those who saw it coming: "His tools just stun you, and he's coming into that age range when players are at the top of their game." For one thing Pippen's numbers in scoring (up to 16.5), rebounds (6.7), and assists (5.4), had become those of a true star who carried a championship team, and not those of just a supporting player.

The Bulls finally stood on the verge of their first-ever NBA championship. The season that opened in November 1990 seemed to be their time of destiny. Everyone around the NBA seemed to sense that Michael Jordan was finally about to win his first and long-awaited championship ring. But there was another feeling around the league as well. It was the feeling that the Bulls' Scottie Pippen was also about to become a major prime-time star.

Chapter 4

Sometimes it's not all that bad to be number two. A runner, race car driver, or swimmer can pace himself or herself from the runner-up position and then make a sudden move past the leader down the home stretch to snatch a surprise victory. A star player in any sport can also develop more easily when remaining out of the limelight and away from the pressure of publicity while his or her talents gradually mature.

Scottie Pippen did just this. He remained in the shadows and quietly perfected his game and his talents. Pippen's scoring average steadily improved during his second (14.4) and third (16.5) winters in the NBA, as did most of his other statistical numbers.

There was another great advantage to playing on a team with Michael Jordan. Once help arrived in the form of the talents of Pippen, Grant, Cartwright, and others, the Bulls were clearly a team destined for greatness. Even while playing in Jordan's shadow, his teammates had a real chance to achieve every pro basketball player's ultimate dream—winning an NBA championship.

From the opening week of the 1990–91 NBA season, it was clear that the Bulls had zoomed to the head of the class. They not only enjoyed one of the league's best records throughout the entire long season, but they broke many team milestones along the way as well. Between mid-December and late March, the Bulls enjoyed the longest home winning streak in franchise history, capturing twenty-six straight games in Chicago Stadium without a defeat. February saw the Bulls post an 11-1 record for the best month in club history. By the end of the highly successful season, the team had won over sixty games for the first time ever and had also captured Chicago's very first division championship.

The spectacular regular season of 1990–91 enjoyed by the Chicago team of second-year coach Phil Jackson seemed to send a message all around the NBA. That message indicated that a new talented team was now ready to replace the Celtics, the Lakers, and the Pistons at the very top of the pro basketball world.

Michael Jordan was no longer getting all the praise on this new and improved version of the Bulls. There were many who also argued that this team owned not only the single best ballplayer but the two best ballplayers. Veteran observers and dedicated fans alike were suggesting that when it came to the league's current players, and when the issue was a complete package of offensive and defensive skills, Pippen ranked no lower than number two.

Pippen had by then not only become a great individual player, but he was a player who made his team much better as well. He had filled out to 210 pounds and now was muscling opponents under the boards as well as racing up and down the court as a fast-break specialist. His scoring was up to nearly 17.8 points a game. And it was Pippen who almost always drew the task of defending an opponent's very best offensive

Phil Jackson became the Bulls head coach just as Scottie Pippen's career began to take off.

player. Pippen was also playing all over the floor at the offensive end, sometimes in the role of point guard, sometimes as small forward, always attacking other teams' defenses whenever they started to concentrate too much on stopping Jordan.

Some of Pippen's performances started looking more and more like those of Jordan himself. In one game against the Los Angeles Clippers, Pippen performed what is called a "triple-double" and valued as the indication of a terrific all-around performance. The triple-double meant that Pippen scored in double figures with 13 points, rebounded in double figures with 13 boards, and handed out a double-figures number of assists as well when 12 of his passes set up baskets for his teammates.

Pippen's play had improved dramatically. It may have been in part because the Bulls' star had changed another feature of his basketball lifestyle. Late in the 1990 season and during the playoffs Pippen had been troubled by migraine headaches. When a doctor suggested the problem might be eyestrain, Pippen began wearing glasses when he wasn't playing basketball. The change seemed to work wonders as the headaches disappeared and Pippen's game improved.

The Bulls entered the 1991 post-season play with the second-best record in the entire NBA. Only the Portland Trail Blazers had won more regular-season games than had Chicago. But the playoffs are a fresh start. The Bulls were inspired to chase after that championship that had always seemed so elusive in earlier campaigns. The first roadblocks would be the New York Knicks and Philadelphia Sixers in the early playoff rounds. The Knicks were easily swept aside in three straight games. And though Philadelphia did manage to win one game, they didn't offer much resistance to the Bulls' steamroller either.

For the third straight year, Chicago would have to face off with the rival Detroit Pistons in the Conference championship round. But this year it was a very different and much improved Chicago team. And it was also an aging and tiring Detroit team. The series was over almost before it started. The scores were all fairly close, but the Bulls swept Detroit in four relatively easy games.

The final victory over the Pistons did much more than merely launch the Chicago Bulls into the NBA Finals for the first time in the history of the team. It was also a game that demonstrated that this was no longer a team carried by Jordan alone. Jordan was indeed the leading point maker with 29 in the final contest for the Eastern Conference title. But Pippen chipped in with 23, while Grant with 16 and Paxson with 12 also contributed in a major way to the scoring. Michael Jordan himself was quick to tell reporters after the game that it was Pippen and Grant and the rest of the great supporting cast that had turned the tide against the previously unbeatable Pistons.

Now there was only one large mountain to scale, one large hurdle that stood between Pippen and the other Bulls and their NBA championship rings. That hurdle would be talented playmaker Earvin "Magic" Johnson and his veteran Los Angeles Lakers outfit. Johnson had become an aging star. He had been the biggest winner in the league during the past decade and many considered him to be perhaps the best all-around player of the modern era until Jordan came along. Johnson and his teammates were indeed aging, but they were still quite dangerous. The Lakers under coach Pat Riley believed in themselves and believed another NBA title was theirs simply for the taking.

At least for the first game of the championship round it did look like things would fall the way of the Lakers. The first game went down to the wire. A last-second three-point shot

Magic Johnson ranks as the best playmaking guard of the modern NBA era. Scottie Pippen and the Bulls faced Johnson and his Lakers in the memorable 1991 championship series.

by the Lakers' Sam Perkins stole the game away from the Bulls on their own home floor. Jordan had a final chance to salvage the game but his dramatic shot just wouldn't fall.

But then the Lakers ran straight out of luck. The Bulls rolled behind Jordan and Pippen almost as easily as they had against New York, Philadelphia, and Detroit. It was Scottie Pippen even more than Jordan who seemed to turn the tide and key the Chicago comeback in the second game. Scottie scored 20 points. But more important by far was the excellent defensive job he was able to do on the Lakers' ball handler, Magic Johnson. Johnson couldn't beat Pippen's defensive pressure and had to settle for only 4 baskets in his 13 shot attempts for a final total of only 14 points. Pippen also made it very difficult for Magic to operate as an effective point guard and to set up his teammates for inside shots.

After Pippen's brilliant defensive job on Magic Johnson, the Bulls had a full head of steam and rolled to three straight easy victories. At last Chicago sat on top of the league as NBA champions.

It is of course one thing to win a championship in professional sports, but quite another thing to defend a title. Repeating championships was especially difficult in the NBA. In recent seasons the Lakers and Pistons had each won two in a row. But they were the first teams to repeat since way back in the 1960s when the Boston Celtics had owned pro basketball and had won eight straight titles.

But once the 1991–92 season was under way it seemed that things were only getting easier for the Bulls. The team raced through the regular season with an incredible 67–15 record. It was one of the best records in the history of pro basketball. And it left Chicago ten games better than anyone else in the league that year.

B.J. Armstrong handled the important point guard position for the championship Bulls, feeding the ball to highscoring teammates like Jordan and Pippen.

As the Bulls got better, so did Pippen. Pippen at long last was getting full acknowledgment for his skills. Jordan was again the league's best scorer, but Pippen was averaging over twenty-one points. Of course, had he been on a team that needed him to be the main man, he would have scored far more. For his brilliant all-around play, Pippen was named to the league's second All-NBA post-season team. And he joined Jordan on the league's All-Defensive team as well.

With Jordan and Pippen both at their best, the Bulls found few if any roadblocks on their way to a second straight NBA title. The opponent in the finals was this time the Portland Trail Blazers from the Western Conference. Portland was only able to push the series out to six games before the Bulls wrapped up another title. Jordan averaged 35.8 points per game for the series. But again it was Pippen who supplied the series' most brilliant all-around performance. Scottie Pippen paced the team in rebounds with 50 and assists with 46. Even skeptics like former great NBA center Bill Walton were quick to admit that Pippen had no peer in the league outside of Michael Jordan.

In two short years the Bulls had joined elite teams like the Lakers, Celtics, and Pistons as two-time NBA champions. It was obvious that Scottie Pippen had benefited greatly by starting his career in the huge shadow of Michael Jordan. But it was also becoming apparent just how much Michael Jordan and the rest of the Bulls had benefited by having Scottie Pippen around.

Chapter 5

Pippen basked in the limelight of the repeat NBA championships. It had been Pippen, perhaps more than any other player, who had provided the balance and extra offensive and defensive strength needed for a championship team. Even with Michael Jordan, it was Pippen's solid post-season play that the Bulls needed to finally become an unbeatable champion. Playing in the spotlight of the championship series two years in a row had also been enough to show fans outside of Chicago how very close to Jordan in skill and stature Scottie Pippen actually was.

But the lives of professional athletes always move quickly from one successful achievement to yet another challenge waiting somewhere down the road. For Scottie Pippen it was no different. Pippen was now a recognized star and a world champion as well, yet fresh challenges lay just around the corner.

After two NBA titles, off-season recognition came quickly to Pippen. He was named to the NBA All-League second team. He was also selected as NBA All-Defensive first-teamer alongside teammate Jordan. But the biggest honor, perhaps, was his selection at the close of the 1992 season to the Olympic "Dream Team" squad that would defend USA basketball honor at the upcoming Olympic Games. Here was not only another post-season honor but a true challenge for the rising Bulls star. What better opportunity than this could come to an athlete who was still determined to demonstrate to the world that he did indeed belong among the roster of the NBA's super talents?

Summer 1992 would be the time for the United States to regain its Gold Medal mastery in Olympic basketball competition. The United States had been challenged in recent years in a sport that it had once dominated in international competitions. Four years earlier, American basketball fans had been embarrassed by a third-place Olympic finish. The Americans had also lost the Olympic Gold Medal in a shocking upset at the hands of the Russians back in 1972. In more recent Olympic competitions and other international matches, the USA teams had usually managed to win, but often by only slim margins over much improved European and Latin American national teams.

But this would be an Olympic competition different from any others that had come before. Team USA had in the past featured great Olympic lineups, like the one in 1960 that boasted Oscar Robertson, Jerry West, and Walt Bellamy. But never before had an Olympic squad—or any other basketball team for that matter—so stimulated the imaginations of basketball fanatics everywhere around the United States and throughout the world.

For the first time, professionals from the NBA would be playing for the USA at the Olympic basketball festival, to be held this time around in Barcelona, Spain. The American team featured all the game's greatest stars and was therefore unquestionably the most talented squad ever put together for

Pippen could soar above the rim like teammate Jordan and even jam shots over seven-foot centers like Indiana's Rik Smits. Because of his immense talent, he was selected to be a member of the USA Dream Team.

actual competition. Alongside Scottie Pippen, the roster of Team USA contained names like Michael Jordan, Magic Johnson, Larry Bird, Charles Barkley, Patrick Ewing, David Robinson, and a handful of other NBA greats. Now the Americans would again be beyond any serious challenge in the game they had long claimed as their own native sport.

Pippen had been one of the first five players chosen by a selection committee, headed by Coach Chuck Daly. Daly was charged with the task of filling out the "Dream Team" super roster. Pippen didn't disappoint; his solid play off the bench in Barcelona was everything that had been expected of Jordan's spectacular teammate. America's Dream Team cruised to an easy championship victory by humiliating a Croatian club that was European champion and that itself boasted NBA stars Drazen Petrovic and Toni Kukoc. Now the entire world had been shown that Scottie Pippen belonged among the world's elite players. Pippen, for his part, had added a prestigious Olympic Gold Medal to his own already growing collection of basketball accomplishments.

It was then time to get back to the business of defending a hard-earned NBA title. No team had won three straight championships since those invincible Boston Celtics back in the 1960s. Although the Bulls would again win their division with 57 victories during regular season play, it hardly looked like a third straight title was at all a sure thing for Chicago. The New York Knicks with Patrick Ewing had won 60 games in the Atlantic Division, and the Phoenix Suns behind Charles Barkley had captured 62 wins out west. Both of these challengers seemed to stand an excellent chance of bringing the Bulls' glory run to a sudden and final halt.

It was a great individual year for Scottie Pippen, however, the best so far in his still-young career. Pippen quietly

Pippen and the Dream Team humiliated the European championship team, Croatia, that boasted NBA stars Drazen Petrovic and Toni Kukoc. Kukoc would try to fill Michael Jordan's shoes after the Bulls' biggest star announced his surprise retirement in 1993.

averaged 18.6 points, paced the club in minutes played as well as assists, and trailed only Horace Grant in rebounding.

Regular season action suggested that the Knicks and Suns were ready to challenge the Bulls for supremacy. The post-season playoffs would find the Chicago team again at the very top of its game. But there would nonetheless be many thrills and even some close calls before the playoffs were over. The Eastern Conference title matchup found the Knicks opening a two-game margin with back-to-back victories in Madison Square Garden. The Bulls then won four games in a row to clinch the series. Yet this would be an off-series for Jordan, and Pippen would have to pick up much of the offensive slack.

The title series with the Phoenix Suns would turn out to be one of the most exciting and most competitive in league history. Jordan pocketed another NBA Finals MVP award by averaging 41 points per contest. Pippen's supporting role was more than enough to make Coach Phil Jackson's Bulls once more unbeatable. Pippen was the club leader in assists against the pesky Phoenix team, trailing only Jordan in points and Horace Grant in rebounds.

The Bulls would jump off to a commanding lead against Phoenix and Charles Barkley by becoming the first team ever to open an NBA Finals series with two victories on the road. The whole series in the end came down to an exciting sixth game back in Phoenix, however, and the title was finally clinched only when Bulls guard John Paxson sank a dramatic three-pointer just seconds before the final buzzer.

The Chicago Bulls now owned a very special place in NBA history. Previously, only two teams had captured three or more championships in a row. And the last of these, the Boston Celtics, had done it nearly a quarter century earlier.

Larry Bird of the Boston Celtics was a forward who featured a complete game of shooting, passing, rebounding, and running the floor. Bird is just one of several NBA greats Scottie Pippen played with on the Olympic Dream Team.

The cheers of delirious fans had hardly died down when suddenly, shocking news hit the basketball world on the eve of a new season. It was the biggest news of this or almost any other season, and it was being made several weeks before the first ball was bounced or the first shot was taken. And that news broke in a baseball stadium, not a basketball arena. While watching the Chicago White Sox play in the American League Championship Series against the Toronto Blue Jays, Michael Jordan announced that he would not be reporting to the Bulls' 1993 fall preseason training camp, which was scheduled to open in a matter of only days. Drained by the tragic murder of his father and perhaps with nothing more to prove on the basketball court, Jordan was giving up the game.

The mantle of leadership had been passed on to Scottie Pippen. He was now left to carry not only the Bulls' fortunes but perhaps the reputation of the whole league as well. The door was now wide open for Scottie Pippen.

Chapter 6

For Scottie Pippen the 1993–94 season was in many unexpected ways a huge disappointment. Air Jordan was gone, and Pippen seemed poised to inherit Jordan's headlines and glory. But it didn't always work out that way. There was indeed a huge increase in the publicity surrounding Scottie Pippen during the first season after Jordan's retirement, but much of that publicity was surprisingly negative.

The Bulls won 55 games in 1993–94. This was considered a fairly remarkable accomplishment without Jordan. However, fans were naturally disappointed when their biggest star left at the height of the team's glory era. Many hoped that Pippen would be enough to keep the proud championship string going. But the performance of the Chicago team would soon itself be the second big disappointment for Bulls fans. The 1993–94 team was still good enough to win more than fifty games for a fifth straight season. But anything less than a fourth NBA title now seemed unthinkable.

The Bulls would also suffer other key losses besides Jordan. First Horace Grant could not agree with Bulls owner

Horace Grant could not agree with the Bulls' owner on a new contract and signed, instead, with the Orlando Magic. Here, as a Bull, Grant slams home a basket against the Indiana Pacers while center Bill Cartwright and Scottie Pippen look on in the background.

Jerry Reinsdorf on a new contract and therefore jumped ship to the rival Orlando Magic before the start of the 1995 season. Later, center Bill Cartwright also departed from the ball club as a free agent. Pippen lost not only his high-scoring running mate but much of his rebounding help as well.

The team also didn't have much spirit left. There were accomplishments that other teams would have envied. When Pippen, Grant, and B.J. Armstrong were all named to play in the 1994 All-Star Game, it marked the first time that Chicago boasted three All-Star selections. And the team did maintain second place in the Central Division and even survived the first round of the playoffs. But in the second post-season round against New York the team floundered. The Bulls' championship string ended in a low-scoring 87–77 game-seven defeat in Madison Square Garden.

For his own part, Pippen did play well enough to earn praise and honors all around the league. His brightest moment was his MVP performance during the All-Star Game. But when it came to winning championships, Pippen clearly could not carry the load by himself. Frustration seemed to build up around Pippen and his teammates. When the Bulls stumbled in the post-season against New York, there were few happy players on the Chicago ball club.

Then came a black moment in Scottie Pippen's career. He refused to go back onto the court for the final 1.8 seconds of a vital playoff game against the rival Knicks. Reports circulated in the press that Pippen had refused to inbound the ball on that final play simply because Coach Phil Jackson had designed a plan that would leave Toni Kukoc and not Pippen with the final game-deciding shot.

Pippen's actions and his squabble with Jackson were perhaps somewhat overblown and misunderstood; yet the incident had nonetheless called attention to his possible jealousy of the high-salaried newcomer, Toni Kukoc. It had also cost his sliding team a chance for an important post-season victory.

The moment added another blemish to Pippen's already somewhat tarnished image. Pippen had drawn similar criticisms once before when he had complained about a migraine headache during Chicago's 1990 Eastern Conference championship seventh-game loss to Detroit. When the Bulls had signed Kukoc, Pippen had first protested the adding of another high-profile star, and then even demanded to guard the Croatian star during the summer Olympic competition in order to prove that he was a better player than Kukoc.

When the Bulls entered their second season without Jordan, the frustrations continued and even escalated. Pippen was unhappy with his contract as well. His complaints seemed reasonable, since he was the team's star and yet only the fifth-highest-paid athlete on the roster. However, it had been by his own choice that he had locked himself into a long-term contract that now kept his salary fixed at an earlier level.

The trouble began back in June 1991 when Pippen demanded a five-year contract extension for $18 million, despite the protests of even his own agent. Remembering his father's stroke and the fact that his brother Ronnie was confined to a wheelchair from a high school gym accident, Pippen had rushed into a long-term deal that would give him immediate security. Although the long-term contract would seem to protect him from events such as serious injuries, it would also clearly limit his future potential earnings. Several years later, aware that some of the other players were being paid more than he was, he felt he deserved a better contract.

Another unfortunate moment came in the middle of the 1994–95 season. Still frustrated by his team's lackluster play and by his salary feud with management, Pippen finally let his anger come to the surface. He tossed a chair from the Bulls' bench halfway across the floor after he was called for a technical foul.

Pippen still played admirably and even his biggest critics admitted that he never let his unhappiness influence the way he played basketball. Fans and experts alike agreed that Pippen, once he stepped on the floor, was one of the two or three most valued players in the league. The best evidence of this was the apparent high demand for Pippen's talents among other league teams. Throughout the long season rumors flew constantly that Chicago might trade the league's most valuable product in order to acquire young players and build for the future.

Then something unexpected happened that ended all talk of a Pippen trade and sidetracked his desire to go somewhere else where he could again be part of a winning team. The surprising announcement that Michael Jordan was giving up his baseball dream and returning to the NBA came just in time for another Bulls drive toward a post-season championship.

The post-season saw the Bulls play almost like the Bulls of three seasons earlier as they swept aside Charlotte in the opening round. For one thing, Pippen seemed to relish the return of his old backup role. For the time being the controversies were over, the media pressure was again on Jordan, and the talk about the Bulls centered squarely on championship play and not on contract squabbles.

In the end, the Bulls did not make it into the championship round. The Orlando Magic with their powerful young center Shaquille O'Neal were too much for Chicago. The Bulls fell in the conference semifinals for a second straight year. But this still looked like a Bulls team of old, one with the flashy Jordan at the controls and Pippen devastating the opposition from behind the front lines. There was hope that a tandem of

A surprising return by Micahel Jordan took the pressure off Pippen in the 1994–95 season.

Dave Cowens was the only player ever to lead his NBA team in all major statistical categories, until Scottie Pippen duplicated the feat in 1995.

Jordan and Pippen might again lead the Chicago Bulls all the way to the top.

Jordan played in only 17 of 82 regular-season games when he returned. It was Chicago's Pippen who earned a selection alongside David Robinson, Karl Malone, John Stockton, and Anfernee Hardaway on *The Sporting News* NBA All-Star team. And it was Pippen who was barely edged out by Denver's Dikembe Mutombo as the league's best defensive player of the year.

Scottie Pippen earned another unique distinction in 1995 as well. Pippen was called on to play at power forward and at small forward, and also to guard the opposition's best scorer. Nonetheless he also became only the second NBA player to lead his own team in all of the major offensive statistical categories for a full season. Dave Cowens had done this with the Boston Celtics back in 1977–78, but none of the league's other great all-around stars, like Oscar Robertson, Larry Bird, Magic Johnson, or Michael Jordan, had ever accomplished such a feat.

Scottie Pippen now stood alongside Oscar Robertson and Larry Bird as part of a unique trio of the game's greatest all-around performers. These were players who always seemed to lead their teams in all three major offensive categories—points scored, rebounds, and assists. These were the all-time "triple-double" men.

As Pippen's ninth pro season unfolded in the fall of 1995, the Chicago Bulls' once over-shadowed star now also seemed to find new confidence in this status among the game's all-time greats. With Jordan returned to old form, and the addition of top rebounder Dennis Rodman, the Chicago Bulls once again seemed unbeatable. By the mid-season All-Star break, they had earned an amazing 42-5 record and were on a pace to post the best regular-season record of all time.

This time around few fans or experts doubted that it was Pippen's team, as well as Jordan's, that stood atop the league standings.

Career Statistics

Year	Team	G	FG%	REBS	AST	STL	BLK	PTS	AVG
1988	Chicago	79	.463	298	169	91	52	625	7.9
1989	Chicago	73	.476	445	256	139	61	1,048	14.4
1990	Chicago	82	.489	547	444	211	101	1,351	16.5
1991	Chicago	82	.520	595	511	193	93	1,461	17.8
1992	Chicago	82	.506	630	572	155	93	1,720	21.0
1993	Chicago	81	.473	621	507	173	73	1,510	18.6
1994	Chicago	72	.491	629	403	211	58	1,587	22.0
1995	Chicago	79	.480	639	409	232	89	1,692	21.4
Totals		630	.489	4,404	3,271	1,405	620	10,994	17.5

Where to Write Scottie Pippen:

Mr. Scottie Pippen
c/o Chicago Bulls
United Center
1901 West Madison Street
Chicago, IL 60612

Index